Hope For Better Future

❖ DO NOT BE HINDERED BY LIMITATION AROUND YOU.

"Learning Out Of Success, Mistake, Failure And Knowledge Of The Others Sometimes Make A Better Beginning, And The Best Ending"

ADETOPE ADENIJI

<u>CONTENTS</u>

About the book

Contents

Dedication

Acknowledgement

Introduction

❖ DEDICATION

This book is dedicated to the almighty God, Who makes all provisions, and to the loved ones, especially those who believe in learning irrespective of the source of the knowledge, and the whole lots of teachers in the whole world.

❖ ACKNOWLEDGEMENT

I must appreciate my loving wife, Tope Adeniji and my son, Tomiwa Adeniji whose understanding of the effect of building my career fell on while battling with the transformation of the better future, my parents, Very Rev and Mrs J.A Adeniji for their support, right thinking of living and consistent believe in my vision. Sir and Rev Mrs A.B.A Aladekomo, Daddy Ayo Oni, Rev Ayo Richards Bro&Sis Akin Leoso and Mr and Mrs Amos Adeniran, The Rev and MrsOlatundeOluwatosinOnadipe for their parential care and the words of encouragement to think often above the impossibilities. My siblings Bro Dapo, Segun, Wemimo, Oyinade and Florence and friends for accepting me warmly the

way I am and for being there to rescue
whenever things fall apart. Diposobande,
Tope Adegbite and whole lots of friends
for their inestimable contribution and
worth of value to accomplish the goal. I
pray that God will bless you all.

❖ INTRODUCTION

To have a standard Nation well-built and an economic reform, there is premier need to ameliorate the worsen poverty range and ratio, and more so, to fascinate and thrill the inner potential of the populace to be awaken to regain their right and dominion. Sincerely, without having an impact in life, most especially in the lives of those who believe in the intrinsic worth of knowledge and its importance, my effort so far as regards the words of exhortation and facilitation cum dynamics in music are aborted.

I have pasted several of my messages on the face book "topeadeniji@facebook.com", while the responses and the feedback so far were encouraging and showed that, a lot of people are thirsty of our school of thought. Many have demanded for the compilation of our books both within and outside the nation, and we have made a promise that, it shall come to pass to comprehensively have them. Our mission however is to explain and give a documentation of the thousands of our work, that is, words of exhortation, facilitation and music in a more pellucid and explicit way for the benefit of our generation and the generation unborn, to be more enlighten and orientated in our own capacity and thinking strength ability to be able to determine their purpose and mission in an attempt to be fulfilled and to gain a full insight to their emancipation and liberation at all cost.

In our first album, we discovered that our intention was not given the due worth in relation to the merging of the songs and the words of exhortation which many counted to be child's play or a regular artistic work other than being able to decode our real plight of passing across knowledge and information. However, this has made us to look at the separation of the two similar but different kind of avenue of disseminating the information at the angle of verbal and writing, and singing.

Initially, my intention was to go into lecture room in the higher citadel of learning in any of the related discipline in line with my course of study but I eventually considered that, way of life is more pertinent to relate on at this dispensation of difficulty and uncertainty to have a competitive standard of living.

Our explanation and briefing are concise and snappy because, of the value of time and for the sake of those who do not have passion for vast reading and as a result of numerous other topics to be treated.

"The cap that does not fit another man is another man's size" Many have regarded themselves as a failure and of no importance as regards the various encounters they have experienced either directly or indirectly while they live. Many think that, there can never be a way forward anymore as regards seeing the so called mighty in their definition of their qualification, who probably is more qualified than them, exposed, richer or of good academics report failing or unproductive. The simple analysis is that what someone is cannot be what another person is. The best a man can do is never the measure unit of what another man can do.

A man should never admit in his philosophy and thinking of the power of impossibility or restriction even when it seems there is complexity to achieve but under must, he must perceive the impossibilities as possibilities. Many are unable to attain their respective goal and objectives just because of the negativities and discouragement associated with their environment. It is however necessary for all to have the cleared understanding that, human being were created to find solution to the issues arising in their respective quarters and immediate environment. To be candid, an environment without challenges should be deserted and make not worthy of living.

In my findings, I have proven that one of the major restricting elements of success is the undue consideration of other people's inability and failure as a yard stick to one's capability. While in the academics environment, most of the students believe not in what they can do, but most at times, they conceive the ability of the others first before having the courage to react to their subject. They have the notion that, if a subject is difficult for anyone among them with an academic excellence as a result of his input to the studies, there might not be an advantage to excel on such a course.

So also, when the result comes out, if such an individual that has been placed high as a result of their lackadaisical demeanor to studies should eventually fail, they consider themselves failure, whereas, most at times, reverse is the case. There is need to determine yourself and your value to do mysterious wonder and amazing things. There must never be an attitude of I cannot do in the life of anyone that purposes to have a break through. Whatever is the result of anyone around you as a result of his involvement in any undertaking should interpret to you of your differentiation in quality, value, ability, dream, idea, tactics and capability to be exceptional and to excel. Do not be timid or panic of the things around you to devalue your worth to success.

The whole essence of the book is however that, what someone cannot do should be what someone else should do, and if I am not mistaken, what you have probably find difficult, or that someone had failed to do should be your priority to have an added value to living. This however brings the beauty and the uniqueness in you and spring forth success and notation to arrive in life. Other people's deficiencies should however never be termed as a discouragement to growth and development but a learning point to be where you are destined to be. This brings about the separated destiny, attributes and qualities implanted in each a human.

It is of my interest to relate on few of the sub topics to furnish the readers more on the insight and clarity of view to have an effect in the lives of the set of individuals living dependently on the paste of success or failure of the others.

Conclusively, the book will concentrate on the best in another man does not measure the best of what you and I can deliver or do but, to understand and be familiar with various level of performances in relation to the best you and I can do. We have an album titled "The Light Of God" that contains songs and words of exhortation that leads to the foundation of our structure which is Truth, Light, Justice and Reality in verbal communication and singing. Hence, here comes the release of the book "Never Be Hindered; By The Limitation Around You. 'Tope Adeniji.

<u>Chapter **one (1)**</u>

❖ ABILITY AND ITS CORE USEFULNESS.

There is no man that has ever been made without a unique ability or the other. What a man cannot do, can be learnt, but the position of the heart and the willingness of the human either allows them to move on or descend in their respective issues to be resolved. Your ability is developable and can grow if you want it to actually be.

Take for instance, there is no man that understands his features and qualities at the point of his birth, no one knew the day he was born if he is not kidding. Everyone has something so spectacular and different to accomplish or to do in life. The direction of your interest with what you can imagine or what are in existence in your environment connotes who you are and what to be. If at a stage, you realized the need to adjust, you can make u turn to have a better living if only you have made change not your enemy.

It is indeed needed to understand the meaning of the word ability, to have a better understanding of the subject matter and to be able to flow in the direction of my reasoning while having a connection in the line of my analysis and expression. Ability is simply regarded as the capability and the internal or external strength to carry out a function. It is an enabling element that gives an input to the progression of an outcome in relation to the pre tangential purpose.

It is the willingness to grow the inbuilt and innate product that makes a man to influence or adjust activities. It is a common value in man to exhibit a certain purpose or event to arrive at a projected figured out vision and intention. It has to do with the trend of flowing and how convenient it is to adjust in a circumstance to regain a mission. It can be said to be an act of giving trial to the condition revolving around the globe of the world to create and re-create a distinct and unique experience which turns out to what improves and enlarge one efficiency and mentality.

The ability to carry out all functions of all kinds are however input into all the human at the point of creation but they can never be useful not until a man is willing to put them into use and fully exploit them. The best you can give to an event sometimes have a meaningful result on the best of your expectation. When you are fully loaded with vast ability and you cannot operate on them, it turns one to someone of no importance because ability not used can be disability.

Take for an example, if someone can fight very well, and every now and then fight on the road with the people, he will end up being jailed or being penalized for the assault and notorious act, whereas, if he can fight, and he is registered and approved fighter on the ring, he will be paid and not only that, he will be recognized. What I am saying is that, your ability is to make you and not to destroy you. If a man thinks often on what he can do but yet he has never made any provision for himself to do it, then, all his effort are made to be futile, not only that, his time is wasted on irrelevant which cannot add value but a defect on him.

With the explanation to make a reasonable deduction out of the point I am trying to derive, I want to say at this junction that, your ability makes you to have two optional choices to make in relation to the actual place of your operation. In essence, your ability either classifies you into the first phylum or the second class which can be extracted from my own school of thought as regards the economic functionality that leads to either success or failure of a man.

The first class is sole economical function. This is an instance at which a man makes bedrock of having a personal operational value to provoke the inbuilt ability he has to spread in term of his dream to sustain his living and to affect his income and wellbeing. This is sometimes term as sole proprietorship and self-employed business. This marks the ability to give the very best of yourself for your economic developmental activities.

On the other hand, the second class is indirect economical function or employee. This is the angle at which many conceived that they can have a break through either through working permanently or working for the time being for the capitalization and saving's reason to be able to opt out to the first class aforementioned. But it is somehow very complex to have a change in this scenario as a result of the fear of the unknown that eliminates a lot in such a decisional and discretional attempt.

Whatever the phylum a man finds himself, the most paramount is for him to know how to make his plans working for him till he attains the first class which must be the end you return back to after the entire struggling of maintaining a reasonable standard of living.

No matter what class you operate, all the essential attributes are already present in you to be able to meet up with the standard as laid down for the purpose of the economic function and you have all it takes to give the very best of your effort to excel if you are willing to be humble to learn on the field of operation of your gazette and you admire correction, adjustment and transformation.

No man is made or created in a way not to be able to compete or transcend another one in his way of operating but the limitation arrives as a result of the best of exploitation of ability and talents which thereafter creates the various level of placement at which individuals find themselves.

Human ability is however to make them and not to mar them, to create an avenue of ascending to the desire height and realm for them to attract the attention of the others to the uncommon generation of the result of their dexterity and to be able to gain a stand in relation to what they have to offer that others find difficult to do.

Not to deviate on the track of our notion and school of thought for consideration, that is, never be hindered: the limitation of another man is your core strength to succeed, it is needed to understand that break through and excellence are never what a man cannot attain, but that which you have no personal interest and readiness to have.

Therefore, the need to have an urge and passion for an exceptional trait and functionality in exhibiting your components and values to be well placed and more so, to have a privileged ahead of the others in term of economic, physical, income, standard of living, freedom, spiritual, mental, and thinking performances. Not only to be able to gain liberation, but to be noted and be remembered for the magnificent work done. These are the analysis and the brief interpretation of what ability means and its usefulness towards the aid of the upgraded consideration of our motive in the book; do not be hindered by the limitation around you.

Chapter **two (2)**

❖ EACH MAN WITH HIS UNIQUE TALENT

There is no doubt in the statement that each man has their unique talents. There is never a man without a special value and quality that is not separated from the others in term of comparison and contraction. If this is the situation and the nature of the human's composition: then why the need not to fully utilize the component in the men for breakthrough in life? If each man have what it takes to live, what it means is that, each a man is essential to another to live, and that each man are opportune to be great.

No one can live in isolation, no one is an island as a result of the inter dependency and coexistence which must occur in the context of living which is a must to balance the living. This however stipulates the importance of you and I to fit in into the gaps as the nature created for all of us to excel and to be recognized.

The irony of life is that, often, men detect and see the avenue in which their respective characters match but might not give a due meaning to the opportunity, either because they are too occupied in their heart or probably, they are forming too busy or as a result of their incompetency or lackadaisical attitude to react to such an events or the ability to conquer the fear of the unknown.

Sincerely, not until a man is represented at a place he is important or needed, his purpose and mission might be redundant and void. Hence, the need to find yourself out in the midst of the multitude and the surplus opportunity to enhance and connect with your redeeming wasted value to be victorious.

Many have asserted that they have no unique value and inbuilt talents, but that can be irony in the sense that, discovering that you have no talent is already a signal of being able to detect oneself and this when improved on, can be translated to discovering others. If the work of discovering the problems is the only obligation you have found to do, you will without no doubt believe with me that the eventual result will surely make you out, if only the intelligent quotient is appropriately applied when due to build you. I must be sincere with you, a man that knows what the cause of his problems is, has made at least half of the solution to his problems. Many are on the street because they cannot identify their problems and what they desire. Most of them can become what they wish if there is an avenue to determine and discover. If your scope is not too expanded than discovering issues, I can tell you authoritatively, that, you will surely be one of the identified individuals to succeed if you can react appropriately on the little but mighty value. Therefore, mere being versatile in the manner of this nature makes you a problem finder and a detector, if you can be very diligent and energetic to the talent's up-bringing and development.

What I am trying to make out of my point is that, you are extremely relevant as an individual than what probably you have made yourself to be as regards your laziness to be involved in the several opportunity surrounding you and not until there is a reasonable contribution to giving yourself to the opportunity surrounding you, one might not be able to have the exact true picture of who he is and his worth. Some people are identified with the way they bully and shout even when there is no cause for such. What I want to say is that, if only a man can be very prudent and desires to be relevant, he can struggle add to have placement as regards what he does. Any talent or feature that cannot make a positive contribution to one's life is a burden in the whole essence. I found it very difficult and amazing to hear what the footballers around the continent earn as a result of discovering their talent and worth on time, not only that, but they are able as well to direct all their effort on what they know how to do to entertain others and to make their living. What most of the footballers earn monetarily is so vast that, some of the president of the nation might not earn such, not to mention the managing director in some organizations. Another sector which was formerly counted as a rejected industry or what people do not like their children to have anything to do with is the comedy, while this has become a hot cake now. Check out the music industry also to see how geometrically people are multiplying in value and worth. What I am trying to say is this, the very attribute you have is enough and more sufficient for you to live with and to have a way forward in life. Do not underestimate your talent. Never look down on what you have. What you have can make you who you are to be if you are diligent and purposeful to attain your dream through the full use of the innate and the acquired knowledge.

You are already with what can make you, what can introduce you to the world and what can take you to the next level when you are set to make the full utilization of your talents and you are set to exhibit what you have. Whatever a man has but not displayed or used are not useful for the ascending to the next stage of life. Count not on what people have said about you, do not think on the past failure either by you or others, but be prepared to make the little light you have to shine and to be seen. Your position, place of abode, country, nature of work you do and hidden place you live has no meaning on who you can be if you can get it right, the rightness, innovation and the efficiency will locate you out of your embarrassing situation and your hidden places when you are set to be refined and utilize what you have. Someone disability and inability should make you relevant. Never be discouraged or be prevented from what you can do as a result of someone's deficiency, for you have a better and a greater purpose and dream to succeed. Ability is never based on what another man does but it is based on what you are set to accomplish. You have all what it takes you to be a man of your choice when you are out-rightly prepared to be made.

<u>Chapter **three (3)**</u>

❖ **WHAT MAN CAN DO IS NEVER MEASURABLE**

What a man can become, what he is or what to be in the nearest future is never what a value can be placed on or apportioned. The only value that can be evaluated is the immediate function which might not give the true best of him. In most African countries, many have various attributes, but they apportion faults to the bad economic situation for not using them, this can be said to be a flimsy excuse. The problems around you should make you of better worth when you know how to penetrate, also, any value not displayed or exhibited amount to nothing, and cannot be measured. The values of men are so enormous that, they cannot be adequately measured but they can be witnessed and examined at a point of their discharge. A man may have thousands of values and yet due to the constraints or condition of his operation and engagement uses only one. It takes a deep thought and processing to understand the nature of human and yourself. The ability to think vigorously above the problems at hand and to understand the trick of overcoming the problems instill in human's concern and thought the newness of the diversified ideas or optional attributes that enlarges them and increases their potential when there is willingness to excel. As a man, the end of a journey must begin another, and this is simply how available the willingness and the attributes of men are set to be operated. The point here is that, there are thousands of talents and skills in a man which are refrained and hidden as a result of the limitation in their application, which however make the real value of men questionable and unascertained.

The only quality that can be established or evaluated are the ones exhibited or displayed at the course of discharging a responsibility while the others which are silent but salient and of better value might not be captured till they are utilized. This however brought the idea that human efficacy and attributes are not measurable, but that which is in use and sincerely, numerous of the efficacies are buried by men.

Examining the plenteous skills and talents of men, they are the sources of expansion and advancement towards the projected proposition of the set goal or plans of the men. However, since it is then the conclusion that the skill and talent of men are numerous and unquantifiable and that each man is recognized with a unique feature, then, it invariably means that the issue of inability to excel or have a break through should desist in our world and that, the inability of the others in their respective inadequacies should be a plus to others other than person in question, also, this must translates to the greatness of their feature and character when the values are well managed.

What a man can do or carry out are plenteous to the tune of having not a specific record for them, but their possession of what they can do is only limited to the courage to apply their traits and inbuilt capability to have the expected result. There must be a continuous pressing further and forward with the assurance of making the very best out of the uncountable human's composition not to be hindered in any way towards excellence. Tap into your resource to be made and to be a champion. If you have been condemned on a certain issue of performance, never be condemned, but realize the need to make use of more of your worth and values/ potentials to do extra ordinary, and to be ahead of the others. What you have can be converted to surplus of diversified units to make a whole and to count you worthwhile.

<u>Chapter **four (4)**</u>

❖ THE BEST MAN CAN DO CANNOT BE IMMEDIATELY VALUED.

Do not have the impression that probably because you have been given the very best of your ability on a certain subject matter and yet you have not seen the best result means that you are a failure or considers that, that measures your worth and value. What makes failure is never the inability to fulfill destiny but the inability to be very persistent and resilient on the course of having a result. Sometimes, human ability are measured in a gradual systematic order, this automatically means that, the little beginning of any of the commitment is relevant and should not be despise but must be made very relevant to form the structure that brings about germination and growth to the highest degree of the intended order.

While in the secondary school, I was able to have a relationship with various types of friend and candid, while growing, I still have the opportunity to have contact with some of them as we move on. The one of the interest as regards this subject matter is the one who all through the secondary school days was unable to be made. He was at all times lacking or being placed outside the circle of the brilliant ones. But to my surprise, we were in The Polytechnic together and in the same level. I was so astonished by his performances right away from the beginning of the first semester till the end of our journey in the school. Someone that was at all times outside the circle of honor, made it his place of abode. Though then, he studied vastly without the impact of the studies on his academic performances but the moment he realized his worth and value, he discovered himself, he was able to put into action all abilities that are redundant in him to have the very best outcome to be exceptional in his academic record. It is quite impossible to make use of your potential when you are yet to discover yourself, it is impossible for you to know that what you can think is what you can achieve when you do not have the mind set of accomplishing them. A man must never underestimate himself or devalues his worth to attain the stage of his full expectation. This view however buttresses the idea of the inability to measure the worth of men in a sudden, but in gradual as there is growth and development to create the proposed pre intention.

What I am saying is that, most at times, some projects look so untidy and not solid but have a good ending eventually. Project is the best comparison in its nature with life in its real sense. A project can be fully germinated within a limited time period while the other can take a very long time period before their maturity stage. The set of project that do not feasible within a short period of time however are condemned and rejected before they are made most at times, and most often, they are worthwhile in nature.

It is not how far it takes a man to be made that constitutes a man but how well; a man should never be crushed or rejected while coming forth with his project or plan, projection and planning requires time to effect it, if truly the mission is giant, but must not take you the entire years of existence to dramatize it, this means that you must be considerate of the time, time cautiousness must never be separated from the motive of a man to be able to actualize the prepared intention and attain the desire level of degree of honor. A man should never be compared with another in term of their value as a result of the various tactics and procedures that it entails to come forth with the projected dream.

Therefore, as the result of the argument at hand, we must have seen the need to be very careful to judge and to interpret the outcome of human's endeavor. We have deduced that, the objective and aim of men though similar might not be able to come into being at the same time. We also discovered that, though the plan or idea to be effected looks similar, there is always dissimilarity in the condition of the approaches and programming to fulfill them. It is however not too ideal or realistic to make a comparison of the human ability in connection of the relationship with that of another person in term of the assessment of their immediate value and worth.

<u>Chapter **five (5)**</u>

❖ **THE PROCESS OF DISCOVERING ONESELF.**

Sometimes, it is very cumbersome for anyone to understand his nature. Knowing yourself is never what can be assigned to a single day but must be something studies for a certain time period of time to ascertain. This might not be accomplished if due consideration is not given to it. No wonder many are found in the circle of struggling forever in their lives without finding anything substantial to do. To discover yourself is to know your bearing and to recognize your mission and focus to be where you are meant to be. Though each a human has what it entails to realize themselves but quite pathetic that many all through their lives do not get it right. It is however of my intention to be a helping factor to break the yoke of the inability to open up the inner mind to attain the height of our glory. I have met with several individuals that had made themselves a circumstance of misfortune in life, forgetting that, even if someone has been made a subject of ridicule by the entire world, but he has the determination to convert the misfortune, such a misfortune can be transformed and translated to fortune eventually.

Furthermore, the gap in the determination of who you are and having the cleared picture of the catalogue of the series of functionalities in you makes it mandatory for the inbuilt talents and qualities not to be wasted or passive. In the later discussion, we emphasized on the numerous talents of each a man which as a matter of fact should be in use to set them free and to make out an excellence in them if well put into action. Process of discovering oneself is a bit difficult but it is achievable as we can count thousands of individuals that are excelling and yet to be tired to improve more and more to accomplish. The determination of one's ability or oneself can however be made in the daily activities as mentioned before-hand and the consequences thereof. These are the feedbacks and the reaction that the members of the public or the immediate environment or associate who one relates with either often or seldom give.

I was trying to chip in an illustration in the sub topic already treated. I said, mere fact that one is able to determine himself has clearly shown that, he has the capability to diagnose himself as regards his problems. The moment you are able to resolve your problem in life, you are turned to problem solver. It means, when you are saved, you can save others. In nut shell, the point is that, if you can be able to map out the importance of your life and you can aid them to be fully used, you can be of benefit to the others in their respective area of advancement, and when this is visible, you are already creating a future for yourself, which means that, your consultation to the development of the others is vital. No one cares to trace your procedural stages of your achievement, but have the assurance that, without having what it takes to be where you are, you must definitely be where you should not be.

The process of knowing yourself and discovering your nature emanates at the point at which you observe that you are created for a purpose and as an individual, you have a mission to accomplish in subject to your inherent capability and strength ability. The testing ground of observing yourself is your involvement in the series of activities around you, unlike the other testing that are made in the laboratory. You must be able to look out for the actual place where you fit in to be relevant. It is possible for several attempt to be made prior to the verification, but what I am saying is that, there is definitely a place at which your talents matches. This is the place where your potential can be best proved and where your worth of valuable talents can be examined and displayed. So, the process to discover yourself is an activity that takes place while you live in the world and it is a must for all the individuals to go through the phase required to be who a man should be.

It is necessary for the human to be sensitive to their environment, to be able to deduce a conclusive reference in the aspect of noting down their various reactions that attracts eulogy, praise, commendation and encomium while in some cases, condemnation and criticism are not exempted. These serve as a subject matter of arriving at the conclusion of process of discovering oneself. Just as mentioned before-hand, professionals such as comedian and footballer are the set of features that can be noted in the life of the human and thereafter build on. If a talent is not furnished and refined, it might be at its raw stage, which might be made useless for the intention that is supposed to be for. Being a footballer or comedian does not make you one if your interest is not focus on this. There is a need to add up your little effort to make a different on who you are supposed to be. Without the continuous given yourself and what you have out to the world to see, there can never be an assessment, evaluation and attraction to what you have and what you can do. The sets of the profession enlisted are however in one way or the other extracted from the general way of life while one is finding out the true worth of his life. There is never a talent or value that is not useful or important when they are put to their use, but can be irrelevant when not defined and used.

However, the need to try on several occasion to identify yourself and your talents, and to make the talents working for you to be a deserving personality and uncommon man as a result of the special and unique components that are differentiated from the others. This however should be made easy for the ones that can have a good reasoning to unchain themselves through the wealth of information, materials and education they are exposed to.

Chapter six (6)

❖ ALL PLANS CAN BE ACHIEVED

I have no believed in the saying that, something is difficult to be accomplished. What a man gives to the world or invest must tactically be the response of his result. There is no magic in having success, but success is a friend of those who have the zeal to attain it. The state of mind and the composition of the human have a great effect on the height of their achievement. Some see success being difficult to attain, no wonder they are never moving ahead in life. The perspective of your reasoning and viewing the world in holistic have a wide impart on your destination and your making. When one has made a conclusion that, it is not possible to accomplish a certain thing or the other, then, the negation must surely be vivid on the outcome of such occurrence. When you have the mindset that, it is not possible, then, the impossibility must be apparent and be spelt out in the result of your commitment. Though, a step is to be taken before the success is made, the unwillingness will never make one to realize it, even, when the success you are aiming at is knocking at the door, the door might not be opened as a result of your unpreparedness to have it and the inability to identify your vision and plan.

People often think of the impossibilities instead of chanting I can do it. When a problem is focused on, rather than, the solution to the issue at hand, it becomes issues that cannot be resolved. There is no time period or any engagement that does not have issue. That is the reason why I make jest of some individual that have made relevant issues their enemy. Issues are the element that expands the reasoning faculty of men, and therefore, there must be provision for issue and how to treat them in our daily endeavors. Issues and difficulties make one to move ahead and furnish mind with the competency and enablement to wax stronger to achieve the perceived impossibility.

Anything a man can think of in the spiritual realm is possible to be accomplished. There is nothing that can be made without its spiritual existence and insight. This means, that all the conceivable ideas and thought are such

that can be attained when there is
sufficient ability to discharge them. And
the beginning of the end of an activity is
the ability to think about the possibility in
line with one's reasoning to meet up with
the standard as designed.

Once in a while, I think on the mystery
behind the work of the creation. I am not
trying to compare human nature with
that of God, but to simply tell you that,
without the deep thought, the world
would have been in desolate. But the
work of creation had brought about the
programming and the existence of various
creation in which you and I are lucky to be
one. A mind that cannot think or believe
in the establishment of a purpose pre
designed or extracted within him, is a
mind that moves in the direction of

desolation. There is no one that, in one way or the other has not been exposed to one opportunity or the other that could have translated his life for the best. The few ones that have considered the best use of the opportunity are however the set of the individuals that are at either their destination or growing, while the one on the other hand, the multitude, that have either handled such grace with levity or dealt away completely with them are the ones that are in their stagnancy or regressing stage. However, with the fact that one has failed to utilize the opportunity in one way or the other does not mean that the second chance and many more cannot come or given.

The perspective at which life is interpreted and the structure within her context on how it is managed to have excellence in one's endeavors has a magnificent symbol of character in one's achievement. Therefore, a man must be fully set and ready for the worst and the best of the nature of the world to have a meaningful end result in case of any of the unforeseen mishap or unpalatable events.

To be born or given birth to is never an easy task, you may ask from the sex of the human in bracket, so also to die is more rigorous. Here, the illustration is trying to depict that, both the good and the bad things are always extremely very difficult to accomplish. The hour and the time period that a man however gives to the emanation of the bad products are more expensive compared with that of the good intention that are meant to bring improvement and adjustment on the value to the living standard and the world at large. Virtually, all things are complex to be accomplished, but there is nothing too difficult to be done. Some find it extremely difficult to eat even when they can eat, some, due to the ailments and different affliction, they cannot. Some find it very difficult to relax while some find it very easy to do. To show affection to human of the same sex is difficult for some, while some find it difficult to establish a relationship with the other opposite sex. Reading of the Holy book by the religious members is found difficult not to mention of praying in the morning before the daily activities commence. What I am saying is this, all things are in one way or the other difficult to arrive at, but when you are set to have them, you can get them accomplished.

A man must be prepared to create an activity when due or not, that is, when convenient or not to be able to have a significant living, else nothing will work for him. Rugged mind and resilient heart is the producer of the possibility out of the impossibility. Never let what you have in you and with you make you someone that does not have. "When you have talents and inbuilt traits that are not used or exploited, they will definitely destroy". Talent is like a bomb, when it is used for its reason, it brings about victory and destruction of the enemy, but when they are kept till they are expired in the armory without disposing them, they become a subject to death to the owner or producers. Let all you can see, that no other one can, brings about life afresh with the aid of your talents and inbuilt ability, to introduce to the world the rare and the uncommon features and character which will definitely make you a gem and an initiator of an idea.

Being conversant with positive attitude is like a fuel in the burning fire. It keeps the interest of accomplishing a goal burning till they are met. When a man has an objective or vision to be made and he had made the provision of the necessary factors to meet up with the stated ambition, then, the right attitude of believing in the achieving of the impossibility is quite essential to be able to record a successful outcome.

It is however not ideal to look at the shortcoming of the other beings while cross examining your worth or what you can achieve in life. Looking at the reasoning that nothing is too difficult to be attained means that, before the accomplishment can surface, there must be due provision for the event. The tactic and the systematic approaches of each an individual matters in the scope of evaluating the result of an event. Hence, the need to understand that, if all the vision are well arranged and the mind-set is focusing on the positive end result, then, the end will simply discloses that, the ability of another man is never important in who another man can be or on the result of his projected conceivable ideas.

❖ **PASSION AND INTEREST DIFFERENTIATE MEN.**

Many at times, people tend to get discourage of what they worth as soon as they see someone of high caliber failing or having difficulties on any of the subject matters to be accomplished. The point remains that, what you have passion and urge of interest on are quite different from what another person likes. And as a result of this, it is very possible for such an individual without no urge, passion or interest on a particular purpose to excel or to be compared with someone with the required elements of attaining a motive.

The intention here is to compare and contrast the passion and interest of a man with another man in the context of accomplishing a particular objective. There are thousands of things that dictate the level of efficiency and production in life, in which the passion and interest can never be over looked. This is what makes an idea to germinate independently and voluntarily with a little effort or no effort. Any man, whose passion and interest are not substantial to the tune of self-sustenance, might find it extremely uneasy to multiply.

It's been part of the usual saying that, someone food might be another person's poison. So also is the way of life. What someone likes exceedingly can be what another man disgusts totally. This however resolves to the various kinds of human desire and their insatiable wants.

Whatever a man does not have interest and passion for, does not look real in his heart before the time of its implementation. Your interest and passion makes the true picture of your intention or a view shared with you. Not only the true picture, but the adjustment of the already existing picture can as well be amended at the spiritual realm prior to its manifestation.

Without being able to get the actual place of your fitting and interest in life, a man might not be able to make the best use of his life, and without making the best use of your life, you might not be able to produce substantially. This can then leads to demoralization and devastation of living and reasoning. Many people are excessively talented and dynamics in nature but yet, they found it tedious to have a meaningful result on their performances. They are never able to release their potential at full value to be established when they are yet to be educated either formally or informally. Well, education has the best value in the life of man, because this shows to him more of the exposure and the insight to the possibility which however makes It reflection in their daily involvement, but your interest and passion can be the best teacher to you when your purpose is defined and you are set to meet up with it.

It is quite uninteresting sometimes when a man sees himself not performing despite the fact that, there is normal exposure to either the formal or informal education. There are thousands of things which might be responsible for this sagacity and lope hole which ordinarily should be made priority to have solution to the incapability. No one is incapable, but one can be incapable if he has not made the total self to be put in use. This is an avenue at which the internal human is given the due value to have a change under must for a better future and to make a way to identify human existence.

When you are encountered by someone who does something amazing in your presence, do not be casted down but be thrilled with the performance, to make a solidified conclusion that, within the scope of your capability, you can as well make a tremendous display of uncommon value. What differentiate you and the others is just that value you have which you have not made to materialize fully. Sincerely, this happens to be what can make you to be an exceptional individual and a man of dignity if you can only learn on how best they can be placed and used.

Anyone seen having a good outcome in his endeavor, means that, he has the secretion of having the impression of understanding his nature in line with his potential. Immediately, you understand your true person, you become like an eagle that soars at the stage of no limitation. Seeing a different thing done in a different manner does not means that, something else of your decision to do cannot be made in a specific manner of your choice. Your performances, has nothing to do with being on the same field of operation with another man, but being able to sacrifice and fully exploit the opportunities that are directly in connection with your destiny. Having an encounter with a specific performance of honor simply shows a sign and symbol of empowerment and encouragement. This means that, human's talent are expensive and there is no one that is left out of this feature in their making, and by the way, each an individual are opened up to virtually all the opportunity surrounding them to make out the greatest returns. You talents are more expensive compare with the other individuals you might have an encounter with in life, so let them be well placed to place you, in order not to displace you.

The inaccurate evaluation of men in line with what they have had an encounter with or what they have seen create a wrong impression on devaluing the true worth of human as a fictitious imagination arises to give a conclusion on the ability of the others in looking at both the possibility and impossibility. But at this junction, I want to tell you courageously that, there is nothing impossible when you are set to have them accomplished, but your passion and potential must never be a stake or disused. While thinking or dreaming, let what people can do be the major of your thought, and not what they cannot do, think of what you can do, having your foundation on the conceived possibility of the others. This assists at the paste of success in human effort and involvement in the case of challenges.

Furthermore, the effort is to make a turn around on the discouragement of many whose believe rest in the failure of the others. Do not for once be oblivion of the value in you that many do not have, this makes you who you are, and this is what can change your world for the best. The little thing you do and count irrelevant is what had made someone somewhere relevant to his people and his environment. What you have is indeed all what you need to be a winner not what someone else possesses.

This however serves as an eye opener in the sense that, success is attainable when the potential and values in you are recognized and put into full use. It means that, every other human activities and their result have nothing or less of impact on what a man can be. You do not necessarily need to measure your worth and ability on what someone had done but that can be a simple trace of having someone that had attempted such a circumstance before your time of engagement with it. And if no one has ever attempted what you have to do, it does not mean that, it cannot be done. It is not a crime to have an overview of success and failure but it is devaluing and condemning to pick-up a wrong choice. The potential and value of men are quite essential to achieve the perceived impossibility and to have a rapid growth and development. Hence, a man's decision is important to the height of his purpose and realm of his operation in other to understand that, his interest and passion in whatever he needs to do makes him not to be compared with the another man. A man's ability is not measured based on the performances of the others but based on how the potential and interest are inclined with the proposition.

Chapter **eight (8)**

❖ **MAN OF NO LIMITATION.**

Where someone ability ends is the exact place another person's own begins. There is an aphorism which says, without moving out of your jurisdiction, you might not be able to witness better things. Another one says, when you have not seen another person's farm land, you will think that your father's farm is the best and the largest. If others are not well examined as regards what they do, you might not be able to see beyond what you can see. Innovation, technology and creativity are moving at a paste of high standard of excellence and mega improving in each a day, which means that, the best you can see today must without no doubt be the least you can see tomorrow.

Most at times, the improving rate in human are subjected to their interest which however transparent in their level of achievement. Having interest in what you do attunes the system to the adaptation of the varieties optional decision and changes that thereafter create result. Interest is what makes a man when the rejection and condemnation set in. it brings the simplicity conduct to adherent to the esteemed perseverance and tolerance to meet up with a task ahead. It is however of great significance to have interest to be able to go far on the course of an action, while whosoever that has no interest in his slated dream, though go far, might not be able to meet up with his goal.

Another important aspect of life to be considered to have a purpose accomplished is the vision. The vision is what makes a man to know and understand his bearing, that is, the direction at which he follows. A man must be able to understand better of the things he desires, and must be able to know how to get them actualized. Vision leads a man to his proposed destination, and makes him to understand that, distraction is never a barrier to success when he knows how to handle them. In most cases, people find it extremely difficult to have result as a result of not knowing what they live for and how to get what they want. When you do not know what you want or how to get what you want, then, your skill and ability that are meant to be for the germination of your ideas and aim are wasted and unproductive. This however results to stagnation or regression in motive. Vision is worthwhile to be considered towards advancement and improvement. Therefore, a man must have a clearer picture of his purpose in life and how to get them actualized to be able to be a victor.

Being a result oriented individual is also crucial to have a man. A result oriented man believes in what he does and have the mindset that, what he does will without no doubt fetch him result. We have thousands of men that get discouraged of what their intention is whenever they are faced with a challenge or the other, a result oriented man will not give meaning to what the issues are but wax more stronger to overcome the wave of the storm of the hindrances believing and knowing that, a time will surely come that the vision he has will come to manifestation. He believes in the feedback and the end result of what he has sown or planted, and he is full of expectation of his vision. It is of no doubt that, preparedness and being at alert to have a result and produce sometimes dictates the tune of the success.

Other things that are inclined and associated with success which many individuals count as irrelevant prior to their conclusion that, someone else is better compared to them are, time consciousness, hard-working, dynamism, deep thought, management of resources, creativity and more others. It is however observed that, though, many possess several of these values in a high magnitude but yet, they cannot have their intention in life accomplished. When the values are not coordinated and are not managed in a synergetic form, it becomes an issue to have a meaningful end result. In the context of this, people's disability and inability are never to be a subject to the incapability of any other individual but an encouragement that, the gap in connection with their inefficiency can be an opportunity they have been waiting to get to be made in life.

I am however of the school of thought that, if the individuals that are of high collection of dexterity and values are exposed to the cleared purpose and power of knowledge, and geared towards the level of realizing themselves and their unique worth, they stand a better chance to claim the degree of success and achieving in a worthwhile degree to flourish.

I have the conclusive argument and verdict that, the best a man can do remains the beginning of another man, considering the fact that, all values of human are best put into their use and fully made to work together to accomplish. If an individual can have a cleared purpose of existence and perfect orientation to have the clue on what it takes to be fulfilled and to excel, he will without no doubt be an exceptional entity in his line of operation. However, the best a man can do is never measured by what another man had done at the terrain that welcomes and give meaning to the existence and operation of all the human's attributes. Hence, the ability of a man is not measured based on what someone else had done but on what a man is working on or displaying. There is no limitation for those who had discovered themselves, and are fully set to make their worth and value to work out the magic in their nature to create unlimited realm of operation and functionalities.

<u>Chapter **nine (9)**</u>

❖ QUALITY AND COMPOSITION OF MEN IN THEIR FUNCTIONALITY.

There are several mystery and amazing things that we have recorded from time immemorial till present time. In fact, things that in their manner of creation are so disbelieving, but they are absolutely real in all contesting experimentation. We have experienced quite numbers of identical twins of similar features, but attitudinally, they have no resemblance. We have several sets of individuals that are in one way or the other looking the same, but yet in their character and composition, they are extremely of no comparison. We have people of several wives, and yet we have not recorded a single of a attribute of same like with another necessary but say necessary salt.

Earlier, I mentioned of the different talent and the attribute of men being numerous and being unique to each an individual, this has however made the sub topic, quality and composition of men to their distinctiveness. With the reasoning and the fact that, the quality and composition found in men are quite many and uncountable, we can rarely see two individuals sharing the same degree of worth of efficiency in all the same like attribute if and only if, they have them in common.

What I am trying to say is this, most at times, people left out of their thinking of their possession of adequate substance of germinating in an astonished manner, just because they are never of the consideration of what they worth and the quality lying in them unused. What you do and what you have should be what to give you the due chance and privileged to win and to conquer the battle of nature and its complexity. This is what gives you the internal enabling fortification to pursue on when other relent, it gives you direction when every others cannot see a right at the stage of obscurity.

When quality and composition is defined, it means more than its definition because it defines a man beyond his recognition, in the sense that, your work and innovation and creativity attract before you are revealed to the world. This is the only means at which an expression is incapacitated for reality. More so, the quality and composition of men bring them out gallantly and honorably before the poor, rich and the authority.

Furthermore, it is very sadden and disheartening that, the human magic, that brings diversified talented humanity, self-esteem, notification, identification and improvement to the economic aesthetic and purification is handled with levity and inferior mind, which has made it, the point of mishap to the emancipation of the humanity. We have varieties of opportunities that are existing at each a man's door step that can simply lead to series of discoveries and impartation to our development, people of the greater talent and dexterity find it ambiguous to exhibit what they have, due to the fear of the unknown, which had severely bastardized and paralyzed many dreams and helping hands.

Most of us find it very difficult to suffer for a day to live a victorious life, to be discomforted to determine the comfort zone of revolving. No wonder, many cannot find a way forward despite the fact that, they work like WORK. This ugly incident however is a trace of the poor knowledge and orientation which before now had been in absentia in most of the developing countries, in which my nation, Nigeria is not exempted. Many were pushed to the citadel of learning not as a result of what they have to offer, but for them to be placed where a buoyant amount will be paid even without any developmental effect on the economy.

If most of the people could know their worth and to understand their importance on the range of their respective empowerment and composition, there will be tremendous change in the personal income generation, and not only that, but in the economic growth and development as a result of coordinated system in the world, that makes it more of enabling place for the witty industry or small scale industries/ infant industry to grow. With this, there will however be a reduction in the excessiveness of the concentration on the government's provision while people extend their tenet to different direction with the provision of the social and essential amenities.

The quality and characteristics of men that separate them are what are essential for the nation building in holistic and for the personal improvement when it is given priority to work. When there is a gap in this section or segment, we have a widen hollow of gaps within the context of the economy, and there is always a monotonous repetition and focus on the singular resources or few resources which thereafter erupt the tension of economic decadence. Each a man was made uniquely to contribute his separated and inbuilt talent towards the synergetic performances to the co existence of the living to balance the nature. I meant that, what a man can see clearly in his creative imagination must be what another man might not see, which however, when they are brought to the physical realm bring

about their separation and uniqueness
that adds up to a whole in the balancing
of the world.

<u>Chapter **ten (10)**</u>

❖ **EVERY MAN IS DESTINED FOR GLORY.**

Many at times, people complain exceedingly about the situation they pass through which ordinarily should be what to take them to the greater height but due to their inability to withstand such condition, they are always a victim of circumstance. Yet, they have rejected or probably abandoned what others do to flourish. There is need to have a heart that can strictly encourage one in the time of difficulty to be able to understand the nature of the issues in existence to the nature. There is no problem or difficulty that cannot be exterminated, though it can take years before the due solution is given. Many at times, we find it even not been resolved within the generation that tries to find an end to it.

There are many individuals that have given birth to their off spring and many are still given birth even till the moment, and that is how it will be forever. Out of these incidences, we have not seen any two babies or more coming at a go, either through the natural delivery or the improvised fashion, meaning that, a second or more must separate them from themselves. And sincerely speaking, this is exactly what the nature looks like. There are circumstances, and each of the m is responsible for either turning a life or its reversal, but there is no time period that is wasted. Each a man has a specific time period of his glory, but many of us find it extremely cumbersome to recognize our time. Though you have a specific time for an action to be accomplished, without the injection of the expectant value to ignite the cause of such an action, there might not be activities that lead to the dream.

A man can be of the best fortune and yet, he describes himself as a misfortune in all endeavors because of his insufficiency to determine what leads to his time. You must be prepared, and make provision as a human for an event that leads to another if at all they come independently or dependently. One of the associated qualities of being made is having a broaden heart that reduces amazement and surprise. You may find yourself today somewhere and tomorrow, see yourself in another place. There must be sense of adaptation and adherence to the situation that prevails your moment.

We have all come unitarily, and there is no one without a specific purpose and special character to make his glory revealed. No man without an assignment and his work very clearly defined and stated but, these works are always awaiting the influence of the mankind for their sustenance and effectiveness. Many fail in their journey in life as a result of lack of knowing their mission and purpose. Many cannot even define what existence simply means in relation to their day to day concern and undertakings. Most people do not know that, there is an assignment that brought about the concern on their creation which, it is a must to be fulfilled. There is need to give the necessary attention to the worth and value of life to excel. There can never be anything being handled with levity that can bring about a good fruit. Importance to living is when you know the reason why you are and you can at the same time influence virtually all the condition that lead you there, and that can make you there, which eventually leads you to somewhere else.

What you are and you can be is never what another person can be. Your scope of reasoning is quite unanimous and restricted to your capacity and the depth of your intelligent quotient which cannot be measured by another man of variance in his composition, but due to the various findings and testing can guess but not to predict exactly your next line of action.

Something must lead you to where you are supposed to be in life, and it can either be the good thing or the bad tormenting circumstance. Often, with the records, uneasy lies the head that wears the crown, and that is the reason why, you must not abscond from the processing that refines and defines you. Factually, I want to repeat myself, it might not be something palatable, but an event that occurs when a man runs after the bees to find their honey comb or digging the ground to get a gold. But it is certain that, there must be an event connecting to another before your time emanates, and that makes you to accept the nature and constantly fight on to influence its decision for the best for you.

You do not need to run away from the pressure of discomfort, irrespective of what it brings while you are pursuing your ambition in life. There might not be comfort without discomfort. Things that erupt at the point of forging ahead and having your proposed plan actualized are the product that increases your human capability to withstand whatever the pressure that the nature got to inject on your path. These are the signs and languages of fortification and preparation for the greater days. Therefore, to have the secret of the elements that makes up success and to be able to maintain real level of flourishing in all endeavors, there is need to run through the toughen time that makes one to arrive.

Also, it is noted that people most at times gets discouraged and depressed as a result of their untimely feedback on their life investment. I must be sincere with you, not all what a man sows germinate and not all you do brings result, but out of the many investment you have lies the best to make the best of you to be seen. Success is very swift and snappy sometimes, whereas it takes a longer period of time at the other time. Success is a friend to the hard working, people that believe in it and who can bear long suffering. Without perseverance, your day might not come, without moving ahead, you might not get there and without giving what it entails, you might be who you are not supposed to be.

Each a man possesses their different
ability that is meant to pave way for their
break through and allows their glory to be
noticed. Your desire and I, are however
the chief distracter and hindrance to the
manifestation of the long awaiting glory.
There are various things which you can
see that many others can never see, these
are the things which are predestined to
make you but, when you can clearly see
what others cannot see and you fail to
react to the action that leads to the
encouragement of the growth of your
dream and vision, they will only exist at
the spiritual realm but not at the physical
which automatically means that, its
usefulness is nothing to your existence
and the world in which you live. Hence,
the need for you to work tirelessly to
attain what you have seen to be relevant

to the world at large. This does not affect only you, but affect the uncountable lives that you might not take cognizance of.

Be so speedy and smart to react to you efficacy, vision and dream in life to able to bring out the very best you can be and to be pulled out of the majority as a pole to be recognized by all. When you move relentlessly, you redeem your dying and decaying destiny. Your destiny however proves you outright and glorious when you can afford to give the adequate attempt to your value without procrastination. Creation and liberation is never what someone else other than that whose intention is designed to make it real can clearly explained or proof to the realm of the imagination of the person that conceived the idea. You have the best of the vision and the insight that no other one might be able to interpret in the same like as you can do and have perceived it, and not until you make what you have available to be used, and to be utilized, there might only be something that looks like yours or what you have in mind, but not same like with the projection and the view you have conceived within your heart or mind.

In the nut shell, immediately a man understands his direction and the thing that makes him up, this opportune him of his glory, he will constantly be furnished with the expensive thought and creativity that brings about his standard ability to run into the adventure of the genuineness of his predesigned and predestined purposes which then vividly open him up

to the stage of no limitation or measuring
his potential with that of his other
colleagues or counterpart.

<u>Chapter **eleven (11)**</u>

❖ MISTAKE MAKES A GIANT MAN.

Mistakes are meant to happen in the processing of various undertakings in life. There is no one that is absolutely perfect and there cannot be one except the supernatural embodiment of God. Mistakes and errors are the learning tools to do greater things, and as such, they are the ingredient of power and technological know-how to an avenue that can make a man. They are meant to happen in each a day in as much as people have not decided to quit or opt out of their respective decision to effect diversified activities. The reverse of the intention or expectation is what evaluates something to be wrong or erroneous. However, what is wrong to you might be the best of the expectation of another man. Mistakes and flaunt bring about development and upcoming of event when they are well managed in the sense that, the set of the issues witnessed make it very easy to look at the different types of solution and the need to find a lasting remedy to them. It expands the mental adequacy and intellectual magnitude of psychological and initiative decision.

There cannot be a project without a single mistake of a kind or the other. And the mistakes are not for the jeopardy of the project but to strengthen the enabling components that gives it the best of the options to germinate and to compete and remain for a very long time period. The effect of the mistakes and errors are not only seen in the aspect of their destruction and retardation of the project in which they are made but also, they are necessary for the amelioration and improvement on a specific standard to meet up with the approved and the expected yard stick. A man that is not set for mistake in an attempt to move ahead has not set to effect his decision and view, and he can never meet up with the best of his intention.

Take for an example, the vehicle producing company of many kind of brands must have given a lot of its strength to the creativity and production of different types of nature of kind before they can have the best taste, and having the best production does not state that, there will not be upgrading of the deficiencies on the existing products which can simply be referred to as mistake or error. Though it looks like time wastage and resources mismanagement, but the fact remains that, to be able to compete and promote their work, this particular phase is quite very relevant not to be eschewed. It however means that, at the phase of coming up or relating on meeting the desire of men among which are insatiable, there is need to encounter mistakes and to improve and adjust on them to have a relevant products that are invoke for human's consumption.

When mistake happens, it teaches on the better procedure and escaping avenues on the project at hand and yet to come, because this must definitely lead to an event which will make someone in the midst of such circumstance to know better of the nearest occurrence of the replica of such nature of the issue and how to relate on it to add value to life. I am saying that, when you are faced with a challenge or the other, and you take the challenges to be a learning tool, there is every tendency to know better of on the particular job of involvement. When a man is too mindful of mistakes, he finds it too careful to act, and when you are too careful of error coming out of your actions, it impedes you of acting, which then makes you to be left with nothing to act on. The major way of having expansion and enlargement is to try a certain thing or the other, to try one's all possibility to utilize the available grace to excel irrespective of the thousands of time of falling and rising.

A willing mind to grow, to learn and to create should never be a mind that is so timid to undertake an action though it has an error in it, but be careful of making the unnecessary inglorious mistakes. The elements of either reproach or rejection are often come to being as a result of mistake, but a man must not for once run away from them as they are the things which must take place sometimes before a man can be made. A man can be marred and witness several unforeseen circumstances of opprobrium and condemnation but, the end does justify the means.

As a human, it is demanding of all to be adequately prepared for the gaps that occur as result of our deficiency in coordinating, arranging and management of the resources that were carter for towards a progress or achieving a certain thing or the other as mistake and error form part of our living. At a time or the other, virtually all the confirmed referred successful men have gone through a condition or the other that they did not plan for, but because of their promptness and their consistency towards their bearing to achieve, they however make out success. Many admire success but, they have never sat down for once to consider what it entails. They look at becoming like another person, but forgetting the hard time and situation that such an individuals have passed through before making up and breaking through. If only, the issues that were passed through by the successful men are what men consider other than their affluence or recognition and success, there will be advancement and increasing value to the attainment of success among the men.

Success possesses the twin forces that work pari-passu which a man must be fully prepared for while climbing the height of success. These twin forces can be favorable or unfavorable in their condition to the nature of their availability to be used for a certain project or the other. A man looking ahead to succeed should however be set to accept any of the twin forces whenever they occur in their processing to implement a certain function. My point is not that, because of the inevitable nature of mistake, one should make it to rule over his mind or make it mandatory to occur, but a man should be able to make provision for its existence, to be able to adopt and adapt to its condition immediately its arrives in other not to be degenerated or perplexed on the progression to the desired end. An approach other than the already made approach which is tampered with or distorted must be made to have an existing goal accomplished at the face of any error in association with a pre intention of mind set.

One of the major problem that exist while a man is trying to move ahead in life is the mistake and the error which cannot be over emphasized while looking for the secret of the achievement. They come in a sudden manner, no wander there is every need for the human being to be at alert mentally and physically to admit the unforeseen circumstance when they manifest. As soon as the subject matter is well understood by anyone who is attempting to move ahead, it turns out to be an elevation and advancement instead of its former nature of destabilization and stand stillness. When the mistakes and errors are not properly managed, they turned out to be rejection in all form, dejection at the spiritual and physical realm and displeasure in the term and condition of purpose which thereof leads to the elimination and termination of vision and purpose. This is formed as a result of its multiple existing and reoccurrence of its nature which if one is not resilience, optimistic and full of determination might not find it too easy to overcome such a scenario when they come forth, and as a result might not be able to actualize a specific predesigned purpose.

Sincerely, mistake and error are the sources of fortune or misfortune depending on what approach they are given to blend up the task ahead or at hand. Findings have however revealed to us that, in the African countries and the developing continent, there are often abandonment of project, view and dream when people are faced with one challenge or the other in line with the mistake and error which are pertinent to innovation and creativity. I however want to quickly reemphasize that, error and mistakes are the event which leads to another event of better outcome and gives a thunderous germination, which thereafter leads to fruitfulness and a better result.

Many have been made of the reverse of what they are ordinarily supposed to be in life as a result of their inability to withstand and treat the unforeseen occurrence with due care to progress. When this occurs, and the management of the circumstance thereof is poor and inappropriate, then, the hazard and the reversal repercussion of it is visible in human way of living. Many have counted themselves of lower value and of no importance as a result of running away from their destiny which had been made to come forth with little or major difficulties. Many do not even realize their moment of progress other than the moment of regression, just because of the pain they try as much as possible to eschew.

It is however my suggestion and proffered solution to the mistakes and errors that jeopardizes the humanity to be treated through recognition of human worth and value, and to exploit the full advantages of the disadvantages of the issue and matter arising to bring the very reputable outcome in their involvement and engagement. A man must be well prepared for the unforeseen circumstances and never be moved with the aftermath results of its magnitude of its effect but rather, to increase in all aspect to ensure that all things work together for good on his path way to success. This then, ushers one to the level of full potential and fortification to be more productive and versatile in preparation for the other events, inclusive of the one in which the hindrance is spelt out. Through this measure and avenue, one will strictly determine that, one's ability is gigantic that, it cannot be measured ordinarily if the due demeanor and conduct that lead to success is imbibed, so as to know that, the ability of a man is not rested on what another man had done in the past but how prepared a man is, in his pursuit of success. Learn from your mistakes and make them the basis and the foundational elements to your viability, and not only that, but knowing that the pressure around them are the sources of the wealth of information and insight that creates and re-creates a redefined and improvised tactics and approaches that can make an exceptional result in the midst of numerous other.

Chapter <u>**twelve (12)**</u>

❖ DO NOT MEASURE YOURSELF WITH OTHERS, BUT BE EXCEPTIONAL.

There is no need of measuring yourself with another man. What you are is more important than anything to measure yourself with. Measuring yourself with the others restrict your capability and level of efficiency to performances and reacting to issues. Many look at what others do to determine what they can do, this is the crude manner of growing and ascending to the uncommon height of glory. Using others characteristics to evaluate yourself means creating an impediment to attaining the level at which ordinarily you are supposed to be. As soon as there is limitation and gauge to human reasoning and productivity, there is automatically a hindrance to the level of operation of such of a human.

Sometimes, it is very brilliant and perfect idea to cherish and appreciate someone or making someone a mentor or an individual that someone is eyeing at the angle of his scopes and desire, but the greatest mistake is however the ingénue and disdain influence of this on many on their level of performance which impedes their rational height of performance on their gazette of achievement. As said earlier, this however makes a distance to occur between the real worth of a man and his worth. In a simple language, where others are wanting and are not effective should be where someone else should be productive and exceptional, this make a man to be known and identified and also pronounced him to the world.

A man must be at all times a result oriented in nature. Result is more important than how something is actualized. While taking into cognizance of the procedural stages, you must as well be well informed about what your aim is not o deviate from the real intention. The way someone else reads a book to pass is quite different from the way another student will read it. Each a man has his nature in attempting a particular work definition or an obligation. You must learn yourself very well to know what your internal factors specializes on to germinate, not what someone else does to germinate. What he does and has a good ending on can be actualized also by you, but might not be in the same procedural palace. This is the reason why what you are and have are essential to be identified and be put into action to have a specific outcome of an act that is not common.

In a football match between two leagues, one discovers that their priority is centered on the number of goals they can have not specifically how they show forth their competency on the football pitch. If an opponent is very strong, full of dexterity, have the best playing pattern, well-coordinated, having good ball possession, neat playing and full of other football experiences, these have no value on the match without being able to conquer. Life is very practical and in the real sense, it can be adjusted and remolded in accordance to each an individual's view of reshaping it. There is need for you and I to think on how our own purpose can be attained. It does not really means that, your dream should be undertaking in such a manner that someone else had done it, but there is another way at which the similar nature of another person's accomplishment can be done in a better way. In the illustration of the football match between the two leagues, it is very possible the two have come with the same tactic and approach, but as soon as the match commences, the coach re identifies the lope holes which must be fixed up to conquer the opponents. While planning is going on, the major concentration of the purpose on the pitch is never made oblivion, that is, how to score. Without scoring or having a goal, all other assignments are void and irrelevant. So also is life in her practical context, a man must not be too cautious of measuring himself with the others on their endeavors but trying to be exceptional to be fulfilled as a human.

It is very possible for a man to share his dream with you and his intention is quite dissimilar to what consideration you have given, and it is very possible you have studied a man in line with his ambition and his economic activities and yet you have not really decoded his goal to achieve. You must be able to make a plan that can make your goal feasible, that can sustain you and make you several other optional directions to be made and to be a model. Comparing yourself with the others has no value in what you have to do and who you need to be, but you can learn sometimes from things that are in existence to make out an exceptional product and living. Let the goal of your life drives you around in your attempt to accomplish not what someone had done or achieved, because this might lead you to extermination if at all you do not know what next to do as a result of the inadequate knowledge of determining the foundation of the vision.

It is very compulsory for a man to learn on how to coordinate the several qualities and attributes in him to bring forth a result. Immediately your goal is identified, all the factors within the human system must be made to work hand in hands to bring out the pre planed. There is a need to have a definite goal in life to be a champion. Without what you have to run after, something not necessary will run after you and by so doing, a man might not be stable all through his living anymore. There is something you were made to accomplish, and all what you need to get them done are extremely loaded in you. Have a purpose and be up and doing to get it, then, you will see life with various other goals that can make all things working out rightly well to make you better.

Virtually all things can be achieved, and there is nothing someone else has achieved that cannot be accomplished by another person in a more glorious way. All what a man can think are what another man can think, but in a different direction. There is no one without intelligent quotient and reasoning ability, but each a man focus their thinking on the choice of their interest. And what flows out of their heart makes up the direction of their thinking and that which their internal enablement propels them to do. This then bring out the affiliated tendency of various unique talents and traits at work to display the exceptionality in man. Without being exceptional, who you are and what another person is might not be clearly stated or apparent, and without this, you might not be able to have your true worth generating you the true honor and according you the regards which makes a life worthwhile to you.

Being exceptional is more than being able to initiate an idea or create another one, but the ability to make use of the present system in an amazing nature, to look as if such activity is yet to take place before hand is one of its major features. Making things that are common to look as if they are not at the period of putting them into action is exceptionality. It measures the level of one's dexterity and skillfulness in working with the available resources which either someone had used or not in a complete variation of its use. Identification and re representation of the former or existing in a more adoring and cherish able manner.

Exceptionality has to do with the way and manner things are being done, and as said earlier, its real meaning connotes more than the simple ideology of creating or bringing something into existence but, the ability to relate on the existing to make a complete newness and greater value. Candid, a man should be able to be courageous and bold enough to act and react in particular manner to be able to exhibit his level of potentiality and exceptionality in life.

Many in their composition are too relevant as regards their plenteous loaded characters and their inbuilt genius of bundle of worth and personality, they are always very special in the ways they generates their vision and dreams, but yet failing in their projection and attainment level of implementation because of their inability or discouragement to be involved where they are supposed to be relevant. Without the ability to showcase what you have in life, you might not be able to be fulfilled and to meet up with your expected end. When you have gold in your bag and you have not told any one about it or taken it to where it can be priced and estimated, there is no way the appreciation of the gold can be received from the others other than you. The gold you have in you must be displayed to the people. It must be cost and estimated to place you if ordinarily you do not want to place yourself to where you are supposed to be. The set of the elements of the attributes of men lead them to their destination and connect them even when not prepared to fly. Release your internal strength and enablement to release your life out of the unnecessary hardship and pain disfranchising your liberty.

You must at all cost display your talent, because a hidden talent is a negation to one's improvement and positive shift. Any talent that is worth not having should be released to have another one which can make a man who he is meant to be. Better not to have a talent than having one without being used. A talent possessed but not used is worth as a talent one does not have. There is a need as a must of urgency to be constantly in the haste of giving what you have, which sincerely must without a doubt give you what you cannot imagine, and this can as well be that great expectation of the world, that many are set to witness, which thereafter makes you a relevant individual of prestigious worth.

There is a thin line between success and failure, but the ability to forge ahead or decline makes what your product looks like. A little effort to move ahead or to make sure a certain action is taken on a particular assignment show cases the whole essence of all you have that can make you to live above your imagination and bring you to the stage of adequate recognition and de-abandonment. Your action can cause you to move to the next level and a realm of no competition and controversy, so also it can make you to stand in the midst of the authority and the kings.

The capacitation on understanding the rules of being exceptional which makes one to be at alert, to act in concordance with his instinct to make some certain decision, and to respond to accomplishing them is extremely important to be proactive and qualifies a man to be who he is meant to be. The moment a man is able to step into the height of his understanding of the true nature and the need for him to be exceptional in all doings and dealing amount to the period of stepping into the outstanding behavioral pattern, which thereof make him to move forward swiftly, to be more constructive and decisive in handling situation that induces his human self-esteem of knowing that the limitation of another has no coherent value on his own dominion and break through.

Chapter **thirteen (13)**

❖ THE LIMITATION OF OTHERS AS CORE STRENGHT TO SUCCEED.

In relation to what I have said before-hand, my motive is centered on things which you can do but as a result of your little or no understanding of you possessing them, you are not being able to make them working for your glory. Factually, fingers are not equal is the common language of all, but the inequality in the fingers has made the fingers to be differentiated from one and another finger in sizes, height, function and where they are attached. Your level of academics qualification or education and other factors are though very relevant to your exposure, but no one cares to know that while measuring your achievement. We have recorded several many people whose effort had made them to rule over the scholars and carrying out an exorbitant priceless worth of function through their creativity and imagination adequacy without formal education. So also you and I in respect of our stand to fulfilled our desires and destiny. What had made someone a failure should be something that makes another a successful man. Whenever people are failing or gnashing teeth, you need not to be panic of their terrible affairs but to take heed of the references of their limitation to grow. The limitation of another man is meant to educate another man on how to prevail, not on how to stumble. People tend to consider the fault of others as their hindrances possibly because they can see it from far of, scaring or because of how it took place. This situations are merely only for preparation of a better standard to confront the challenges of life, not to induce or inject the instability and disorderliness.

I was trying to discuss on the type of mentors and their effect on the life before hand in the topic treated. It is very possible the person you have chosen to be your mentor or you have the delight to be, has some deficiencies in him that is either known or not in relation with his performances. If there is any trait of deficiencies in line with his operational processing, and your yard stick is poised on his approaches, it is without no doubt that, such an impediment can be transferred or featured on you as his follower. I raise no objection to the issue of mentorship because I have several people who are worth to be accorded with such a respect and emulating of their philosophical reasoning, but yet, they are not hundred percent perfect in as much as they have human nature.

Your choice in life matters in determining the level of the realm you can attain. Making a wrong choice means, having a wrong decision and restriction in the height at which you relate. Sincerely, there is a need to make a choice on either of the alternatives of the optional values of life if you want to move ahead. There is nothing like, I have no option of choice, if your desire is to do things that are not common and that can fetch you the due weight of your personality, then the right choice must be made.

We must learn how to live in holistic manner other than having a restriction or conservative living. Many tend to restrict themselves as a result of leveraging on outcome, scope and desire of the others which is never ideal in nature to progress and to have an unlimited attainment. There are many consideration of selecting mentors, some to the academics performances, family built or kind, material things, wealth, properties, luxuries, religion, devotion, ideology, believe, theory propounded and several others achievement and qualities. These are however the set of the millions of the properties that should make a whole if one really understand what the nature entails. Not all the characteristics are however supported in the several of the mentors that are taken to be who we observe to be. Therefore, it might not be too prudent to have decided to make a single or few of the elements the chief concentration while others are disused as a result of the standard you have made for yourself in lieu of the mentorship.

I want to have a repetition of my earlier statement that, the deficiencies and the gaps in the living of the other should never be the elements of abortion of plan or make one to fail in any circumstance as it may be in any ramification. But they are just the signal and symbol that exist for you to know better of the preparedness to excel on the issues not accomplished or unproductive before the time of its experimentation. There is nothing that cannot be achieved or make to be if one has the mind set of living above limitation and having a standard above other human defective choices. Also, a man must be in the light of the need not to depend on the few or limited option of adaptation to accomplish a pre- planned ambition.

All what it takes you to grow and to be recognized and not only that, to be celebrated are lying in each a man, but not until they are put into practice and demonstrate to the world they might be invaluable to the existence. Also, all what it takes a man to manage these special features are within them when they are fully set and ready to put them into use. A man must not be discouraged or be panic to effect his hidden genius and at the same time, to realize his weakness and summon the full courage to improve on them. Without such an action taken place, it can be a delimiting and a restriction on the path way to a flourishing living and successful ending.

Give attention always to what people do, their strength and weakness, and let both the two outcome serves as an avenue to be encouraged, learning point, preparation for the complexity to be accomplished, determination of the reality of success and failure, insight to development and improvement, instant of discovering yourself and your value to be viable and to live above the influential natural and artificial limitation.

It is however my opinion that, if a man can be well structured and having the believe in achieving the impossibilities that emanate in his undertakings, there will definitely be several other hidden genius and talents that will spring out and be activated for such a human greatness and mission fulfilling. There will as well be a distinct clarity of opinion that, the ability of the others are quite dissimilar to another and that should not be the best justification of what another person can create when he is willing to make the best of use of all his composition and components.

There is every possibility of getting what someone has never gotten, and doing what someone has not done while trying to make a new life and looking ahead for the better days, and to be exceptional, not only that, but to move higher in scope. Understanding the level of accomplishment to attain the perceived impossibility of life and having a liberated thinking and believe in the special potential which are only reserved for the best in him to be produced, and making the giant in him to be known is quite pertinent and extremely crucial.

Chapter **fourteen (14)**

❖ DO NOT BE UNDERMINED BY OTHER'S ACHIEVEMENT.

Many find it very depressing seeing people moving ahead most especially in their surrounding while their respective purposes are yet to materialize. The achievements of the other individual are not to be a discouraging function to a man that is full of the ultimate intention to create a special world for himself.

Take for an illustration, you and your friends are prepared to have an event scheduled for a certain day in a place not too far away, and your agreement is to meet together in a place prior to embarking on the trip or getting to the destination. Assuming, you all met as planned, and decided to leave for the journey that will take you 2 to 3 hours on 100km/per hour, the journey will without no doubt witness different series of activities which its analysis will without no doubt have a comprehensive historical record. Among which, the various timing of arrival at the point might not be exonerated, though the journey started at the same time, it might not end at the same time as a result of varieties of delay and distraction on the way. Some vehicles will have mechanical fault, some will definitely over speed others while tending toward the place but eventually there will be a cause to be out of the course, while every other delay and stoppage as regards easing oneself and buying of commodities cannot be taken out completely of the journey. Unforeseen circumstance that many do not pray for but which constantly occur, that is, accident might feature, which will either directly or indirectly be attributed to someone or a vehicle within the bracket group.

The analogy however is trying to say that, in the midst of these unplanned events, some will get there before time, some at the specific time, some will be late and some might not be there. But whatever the case is, those that will make it will be there and vice versa. However, the fact to the reality of life remains that, one must not be moved irrespective of things or changes that happen on your track to success, because these are part of the essential things which must occur before having a fulfilled ending. When you have people you have started with moving ahead of you, you must not be discouraged, but possess the interest in finding out what they have gotten right which you are yet to understand, study them critically on what makes up their success records.

Another man's achievement should reposition you rather than throwing you out of your mind set and vision. The series of the activities that occur around you are meant to make a provision for your accurate understanding of what it takes a man to be well built in the midst of the uncertainties. Move on and work harder to be made, even when things are yet to work in the direction of your plan. Nothing can be accomplished without your ability to make them reality.

A man must totally be of himself, and not of another man to do things that are extra ordinary and exceptional. If your control and influence is rested in what others do, it means you are yet to determine what your desiring purpose look like. Your action should be an influence in the world, not having things that go around influencing you if really you want to be unique. The best a man can do should be carefully managed to have a distinct result which measures his level of achievement and relevance to life.

Sometimes, someone may assess another, getting it right in his assessment as a result of the returns and economic benefit at the point of evaluation, whereas, he is not getting it right in the real sense of his evaluation. It might take a man years to have a solidified foundation and unshaken structure which does not fail or falter, whereas, someone whose foundation is not strong germinates and yields so fast in his returns and benefit, which eventually bring forth fruit for a season and thereafter ceases to produce. At each a stage in life that a man grows, he understands his progression to success, but discouragement often set in as a result of the benefits which are not apportioned to their economic contribution immediately. This is often noticed in the African country or developing nations, whose belief are rested on how to meet with their immediate wants and desires. As a result of this, many gigantic and mighty projects are abandoned for the simple ones but of the fastest returns which invariably end up soon.

Every man has in him a spectacular element that entails him to grow, as the adequate provisions were made for a completeness creation of each an individual to have a glorious and wonderful living. Without the full utilization of this, there might not be any function or activity recognized with you and I. For instance, if I have not picked up my pen, gave it a thought and extract what I have in me, the subject matter and purpose of this words of facilitation and exhortation might not be completed, because, though someone else has the efficacy, he might not be able to have same like word for word and idea for idea. While on the other hand, it is very possible that no one gives consideration to the nature of the reasoning to affect lives. Your component should make out your composition to life, and without putting the best of your effort to exhibit your efficacy, your contribution to living and the desire to excel might be hindered and altered.

There is never a crime to look through what others have done or achieved to improve your zeal and passion to grow on your own path. Evaluating a man in line with his achievement does not mean that the same activity should be undertaken, but this triggers one to know that, all things are possible for them that fashioned their interest towards their better future. There is need to specifically know your bearing and destination before you move in life, else, the journey be made without a specific accomplishment. Be so fast and vast to examine your focus at all times to be able to be made. Many live in abundance but yet in the bondage, many in the poverty and lack yet, they compound the pressure of bondage. Without knowing what you want and desire you might not be able to change your position or think of what ordinarily you should have.

Do not be discouraged but be encouraged to see beyond what you can see, where you can see, when you can see them. Let the achievement and the prestigious events around you make you not to rescind or withdraw you on your path way to success, but to add up to you and change your adventure towards a successful ending, instead of terminating your valuable vision and purpose. Never be hindered; the limitation of another man is your core strength to succeed.

<u>Chapter **fifteen (15)**</u>

❖ DREAM ALL THROUGH LIVING.

Dreaming makes a man to think outside the present immediate environment. It takes a man to the realm other than the realm of his living to aspire, look ahead and by choice to plan to meet up with what has been conceived or visualized. Dreaming occurs at the inner mind because what you dream is never what you have established but a proposition and conceiving of an idea to be experimented. Without dream, people perish as a result of their inability to think ahead on how their incumbent problem can be resolved and how a better future can be attained. Vision and dream are tightly similar because they have virtually all characteristics in nature but the uniqueness and special quality that separate vision is, the intention and projection cum preparedness to direct the available resources in the focus of having the dream actualized.

Without dreaming, there cannot be improvement, innovation, creation, technological advancement, development and even a man becoming who he is meant to be in life. There must be an idea conceived that ushers a man to another place of performance. If there is no need to have a special adjustment and change, there might not be need to have brain storm on what tomorrow should be, and if that is the case, there would have been world collapse or concentration on few economical activities to live with.

There is wide discrepancy between someone that can think and someone otherwise. Some people can dream but their dreams are never sufficient in the sense that, as soon as they get to a comfortable zone, they are failing to dream again. A man must be consistent and at all times dreaming to have the very best ending and to keep on moving and excelling. Without this, there might be outdated behavioral pattern and outrageous living. There is need to dream to capture the need and the desire of now and the future. A man must never stop thinking of a way forward in any form of circumstance he has made for himself. Anyone that can think is opportune of dreaming, and even someone that cannot think is as well opportune but might not be able to analyze what he has captured.

There is no one that cannot dream, but the incapacitation between the dreamer and his level of implementation of what he has seen dictates the reality of the dream in the context of the physical realm. Laziness cannot be underestimated as a deterrent to making the dream to be actualized. There is no man that cannot dream, but there are thousands that cannot interpret and analyze their dream, not to talk of implementing what they have seen. As said earlier, each a man has all what it takes to be who he is meant to be. But with the fact that, this is apparent, people still find it difficult to use what they have to get what they want. Human behavior and conduct cannot be totally exonerated in becoming what they are supposed to be in life. Some people believe so much in luck, but I can tell you vividly that, not 5% of the successful men have been made without their designed bearing. When you can see where you are heading to in life, you can be sure of the place to be even while yet to be there, and the material and resources to be used can be planned to be in place to meet up with the desire realm.

Dreaming can exist at any particular place or circumstance in life, most especially at the situation where one is in isolation to have a deep thought and reasoning to forge ahead or to resolve a specific issue or the other. This is at the point at which the inner mind takes over of the physic and natural being. The moment of struggling and combating within the body system to extract the best of the inspiration to act in accordance to the success or otherwise, choice to either remain in the same level or being a failure. Dreaming can simply reveal to you the true picture of what a life should be and gives the ideas of what are to be in place to have such an end result. Though, at the state at which it exist, it has not come to manifestation, but the fact remains that, all what can be dreamt can be actualized when there is maximum focus and total dependent of vision on the wish to acquire them.

I want to reiterate it at this point that, there is virtually nothing that cannot be undertaken or too difficult to be accomplished when you are set to have them done. You can be what you want to be if only you are so sure and ready to be it. Your immediate situation, condition and what you pass through have no direct significance on who you can be in life but your readiness to think, react positively to what you have thought of, to move and to fly make you who you are supposed to be, and your real self, while knowing your ability and value cannot be exonerated in having the right urge and passion to ascend to the level of no limitation and a stage higher than the present circumstance in which you are.

Everybody can dream, everybody have the thinking faculty and imaginational acumen, but most at times, people find it extremely very difficult to make use of their product to make them. Very difficult for some of the students' to know that, if you cannot read and meditate on what you have read, you cannot pass. So also, life is real and practical in nature, if a man cannot think of tomorrow and how to meet with the demand thereof, he might not be visible in existence, and not being able to be updated in his decision to germinate.

Being able to dream is quite different from being able to dream towards a purpose. Our mind is so large that, it can accommodate various kinds of inspiration and thought at a go or at different particular stages of time. A man must be able to prioritize his dream and select the dream of the highest value of order which his agility and potential are viable to make, and out of the numerous dreams, only one or two should be enough to be concentrated on, while every other dreams are made to compliment the selected dream to be actualized. There is no dream that is wasted or a line of economic activities that are not useful at a point or the other. But the manner at which these are presented and defined to the world matters. We have several shoe makers that are strikingly rich, a mere market women well proven affluence and several other jobs like electrician, carpenter, driver, tailor, comedian, footballers and many other economic activities having an excellent outcome and income. I am saying that, the way at which you showcase your trait really matters to where you will be and how the world will accept you. Any dream you have selected must be given a massive attention and concentration for every other dream to assist it to germinate. There must be connection from time to time of the things you dream of when you have made a priority, else, nothing will be accomplished, but rather they will be made in a half way manner. This however has been the challenge of many youth and the adult who found it very extremely complex to break the yoke of poverty or having the capability to gain their freedom. Talking from the experience, at a point in time in life, I found it totally ambiguous to know what exactly I want for myself as a result of thousands of dream and inspiration cum aspiration. But I got to know that, having these options without a definite one or two to perform had turned to time wastage, resources consumption and mission unfulfilled. Knowing this, I had a resounding thought, and this however lead me to my mission purpose which is words of exhortation and music, while other things are in compliment of the mission purpose.

To dream and to have a vision to meet direct the total attention of a man towards the bearing of his purpose and how the inherent values of a man can be directly channel to effects the spiritual language and cogitate at the physical world. It excavates the series of ideas, instances and the remedy towards the accomplishment of a certain decision. Intellectual capability that leads to excellence and the management of the entire components is awaken to bring forth a meaningful representation out of the vanity and obscurity which translate to the hope for the hopelessness state.

There is need to have a dream and to plan on how it can be turned to a vision to make a new world and create several avenues of opportunities for your forwardness. Having the time to dream or making provision for dreaming has no loss of value or depletion on you, but it adds up more strength ability for the exposure that is required to make something out of nothing. When one can dream, he can have solutions and remedy to the problems identified and at the same time carter for the remedy of the interpretation that makes the symbolic reference, activity and function.

Giving priority to dream is essential as a result of its usefulness in being able to spread one's tenet to cover several scopes in a unified manner. This requires giving the nature all what it takes to bring forth its produce which however it is important for the assessment and ascending to the expected end. Whosoever that does not dream can be compared with a non-living thing or mere lower animal that can live and be exterminated based on the influence of another existing living being. There is no time period that dream does not come into the imaginative membrane of thinking of men, but most at times, what we can see are handled with levity. What you can see is quite distinct from what another man can see, and this brings about the incapability of another man to function in line with the reasoning of another man. What you can see and yet, you are not fulfilling might not come to manifestation without you or come into manifestation without injecting your tactics and approaches to make them in right order.

You must not stop dreaming and having a vision to accomplish while living, think on the things that can make you and improve you, not only that, but which can cause your liberation and freedom at all cost. Never depart from the act of dreaming even when things are fallen apart, when seems there is no solution to an issue or there is no way. That circumstance, that leads you to a certain point in life, should be able to lead you to another better place, if you are set and determined to turn it around.

Conclusively, when you can dream exceedingly, you must without no doubt have the evidence and proof of the act and the application of your action if you are set to make something out of your target. It makes a man to be reformed and recreated. It highjack destiny from its decadence and decomposed region to bring glory and flourishing. The secret of the unknown and what people have not considered, and might not consider are revealed to a dreamer at the realm above the others imagination and perspective of their view. However, this is a means of looking above the incapability and limitation of men at the point of executing a certain project or the other in life. Greatness and success are never separated from the person that has formatted his motive in accustom to dreaming and visioning. When you can dream, you can access what other people can notattest and demonstrate what is never common to do, and with this, there can be quick conclusion within your thinking quotient that the limitation of another man has no significance to your dominion and achievement, and the people around you will without no competition and condemnation accede and reckon with your expertise creativity knowledge and innovation to give you the due value and the worth that can commensurate with your uncommon golden injection and contribution to living and world at large. Hence, never be hindered or displaced on your path way to achieving greatness at all cost, there is nothing you can think of that cannot be attained, even what many have attempted and failed on can simply be accomplished when you believe in your potential and put them in their best utilization to make out the real man and

real worth of you. There is need to dream
and have vision, people perish because of
their inadequate knowledge to dream
ahead, to see beyond their tormenting
time period and finding a lasting solution
to the prevailing problems and those that
are yet to manifest. Make a decision to
see what no one has ever seen, and try
the best possible to make them to be
effected. There is enough resource in you
that can make you a special and separate
individual. Dream all through, and make
sure you implement what you have
dreamt or seen, because someone else
might not be able to attain the in-depth of
your conceptual ideology if you do not
execute what you have dreamt.

❖ <u>OUR VISION AND SERVICES</u>

Our vision cut across;

*Words of exhortation and facilitation (Workshop)

*Consultancy (data management and solution)

*Event management

*Classical hymnal orchestral performances

❖ **<u>OUR CONTACTS</u>**

TOPE ADENIJI

+234-803-718-4404 OR +234-808-093-5806

tophyeva@yahoo.com

Facebook- Tope Adeniji

MD/CEO TOPMETHOD,LAGOS, NIGERIA. WEST AFRICA.

❖ **<u>SPONSORSHIP.</u>**

We are in need of the people that can pick u our books in large quantity for the use of the libraries, schools and the younger ones that might not be in the better position financially to have one to study.

You can assist us on publication of our book if you blessed to doing so. Thank you!

www.ingramcontent.com/pod-product-compliance
Lightning Source LLC
Chambersburg PA
CBHW070121260726
48658CB00001B/199